Instagram Influencer and Advertising

A Social Media Marketing Guide Book, Grow Your Personal Brand and Become a Perfect Influencer

Joan Smith

Text Copyright © [Joan Smith]

All rights reserved. No part of this guide may be reproduced in any form without permission in writing from the publisher except in the case of brief quotations embodied in critical articles or reviews.

Legal & Disclaimer

The information contained in this book and its contents is not designed to replace or take the place of any form of medical or professional advice; and is not meant to replace the need for independent medical, financial, legal or other professional advice or services, as may be required. The content and information in this book has been provided for educational and entertainment purposes only.

The content and information contained in this book has been compiled from sources deemed reliable, and it is accurate to the best of the Author's knowledge, information and belief. However, the Author cannot guarantee its accuracy and validity and cannot be held liable for any errors and/or omissions.
Further, changes are periodically made to this book as and when needed. Where appropriate and/or necessary, you must consult a professional (including but not limited to your doctor, attorney, financial advisor or such other professional advisor) before using any of the suggested remedies, techniques, or information in this book.
Upon using the contents and information contained in this book, you agree to hold harmless the
Author from and against any damages, costs, and expenses, including any legal fees potentially resulting from the application of any of the information provided by this book. This disclaimer applies to any loss, damages or injury caused by the use and application, whether directly or indirectly, of any advice or information presented, whether for breach of contract, tort, negligence, personal injury, criminal intent, or under any other cause of action.
You agree to accept all risks of using the information presented inside this book.
You agree that by continuing to read this book, where appropriate and/or necessary, you shall consult a professional (including but not limited to your doctor, attorney, or financial advisor or such other advisor as needed) before using any of the suggested remedies, techniques, or information in this book.

Table of Contents

SMARTPHONETABLE OF CONTENTS

INTRODUCTION

CHAPTER 1

BUILDING THE PERFECT PROFILE

- FAMILIARIZING YOURSELF WITH THE INSTAGRAM PROFILE
- CHOOSING YOUR BUSINESS NAME AND LOGO
- CREATING THE PERFECT BIO FOR YOUR PROFILE
- TAKING ADVANTAGE OF BUSINESS PROFILES
- CONNECTING YOUR PROFILE TO A FACEBOOK PAGE

CHAPTER 2

CHOOSING YOUR TARGET AUDIENCE

- CREATING YOUR MARKETING GOALS AND RULES
- SELECTING THE PERFECT (PROFITABLE) NICHE
- DETERMINING YOUR BRAND'S UNIQUE VOICE
- DECIDING ON WHAT TYPES OF CONTENT TO POST
- CREATING A STRONG CONTENT CALENDAR
- REFINING YOUR APPROACH TO POSTING

CHAPTER 3

CREATING YOUR NARRATIVE

- INSTAGRAM IS FOR STORY BRANDING
- CREATING A FLOW OF HIGH-QUALITY IMAGES
- IMPROVING YOUR PHOTOGRAPHY SKILLS
- RECORDING THE PERFECT INSTA-WORTHY VIDEOS
- WHEN TO USE SPONSORED POSTS
- PARTNERING WITH INSTAGRAM INFLUENCERS AND BRANDS
- EVERYTHING YOU NEED TO KNOW ABOUT HASHTAGS

CHAPTER 4:

INSTAGRAM STORIES

- WHAT IS THE VALUE OF INSTAGRAM STORIES?
- ENGAGING WITH YOUR AUDIENCE THROUGH STORIES
- USING TEXT, HASHTAGS, AND USERNAME TAGS

LEVERAGING THE STORY HIGHLIGHT FEATURE
CREATING LIVE VIDEO CONTENT

CHAPTER 5

BUSINESS STRATEGIES: FROM FOLLOWERS TO CUSTOMERS

TURNING FOLLOWERS INTO BUYERS
CREATING YOUR INSTAGRAM MARKETING STRATEGY
HAVING A SOLID CALL TO ACTION
CREATING A SALES FUNNEL ON INSTAGRAM
GENERATING SALES AND GOING VIRAL
AFFILIATE MARKETING STRATEGIES
COMMON MISTAKES TO AVOID

CONCLUSION

SUCCESS DOESN'T JUST FIND YOU

....

YOU HAVE TO GO OUT AND GET IT

Introduction

Over the past five years, Instagram has rapidly blown up into one of the best social media platforms for businesses to run on. This platform nurtures visual marketing, direct marketing, influencer marketing, and many other marketing strategies that are proven to entice your target audience and increase your sales.

Businesses have been flocking to Instagram to get their name out there, connect with their consumer, and earn massive sales through the platform itself.

These days, you can run a business on Instagram regardless of whether or not you have something to sell to your followers.

If you do have an existing business with products or services that you offer for sale, Instagram can allow you to increase your reach and earn even more sales through your online platform. If, however, you want to take advantage of this, but you do not yet have any products or services for sale, you can use the platform to develop a business as an influencer.

Influencers are individuals who focus entirely on becoming experts at marketing, all while building their own engaged audience so that they can leverage that audience and market for businesses who *do* have something for sale.

Influencers have rapidly become one of the best ways for businesses to get their products out there and increase their sales because they are people who already have a strong ability to effectively market to their audience. As well, it tends to be far more cost-effective for the businesses than other marketing routes.

In *Instagram Influencer and Advertising,* we are going to focus on exactly how you can leverage Instagram to maximize your sales and become a money-making machine on this social media giant.

In each chapter, you will discover how Instagram works, what you need to do in order to capitalize from it, and how you can perfect your strategy to become the ultimate marketing master on Instagram.

If you are ready to grow your personal brand and become a perfect influencer, whether you want to use that brand to create sales for your business or for someone else's, you will discover exactly what you need within this very book.

As you go through, I strongly encourage you to stay focused and read with curiosity, as one big mistake new influencers make is overlooking important facts.

You may feel as though you are already familiar with some of what you are reading about, but understand that there is a difference between knowing and doing.

If you really want to become an influencer, you will have to take all of this knowledge and put it together in perfect harmony to create a brand that sells. If you are ready to get started with this journey, let's begin!

"IF YOUR DREAMS DON'T SCARE YOU, THEY ARE TOO SMALL"

— Richard Branson

Chapter 1

Building the Perfect Profile

The very first thing you must do if you want to leverage Instagram for advertising purposes is to familiarize yourself with the profile and build your profile in a way that increases your likelihood of earning sales.

Instagram profiles serve as a "landing page" of sorts for your brand, allowing people to discover you and acquaint themselves with who you are and what you have to offer.

When you build your profile correctly, you will find that your following increases drastically because people know exactly who you are upon landing on your page, and they can immediately decide whether or not they resonate with what you are sharing.

Ideally, your profile needs to speak directly to your target audience so that they can identify themselves and connect with your brand immediately.

Your profile is going to focus on two unique features: information and aesthetic. As far as information goes, your profile needs to immediately tell everyone who you are and why they should be following you or what they will gain from following you on Instagram. As an advertiser, you should never keep people guessing or have them confused as to who you are and what you do, as doing so can result in them clicking away from your profile and you losing a potential follower.

Your aesthetic needs to coincide with your information to offer an image that your follower is excited to consume more of. On Instagram, your aesthetic is a work of art that you are creating, and it needs to speak directly to the audience you are building so that once they see your page, they immediately know they are interested in it, and they want to continue receiving more content from you.

If you successfully combine information with aesthetic, you will have a page that draws your followers in and has them excited to follow you and be a part of your community.

Note that anything you create in this chapter, you may find yourself wanting to slightly adjust once you complete the rest of the book because, throughout the rest of this book, you will be learning far more about your audience and your chosen marketing strategy.

With the awareness of your audience and marketing strategy, you can make your profile even stronger; however, you do not want to have a blank profile floating around on Instagram.

You should put together something simple to start and then make your necessary adjustments later once you have the rest of the information put together. With that being said, you should refrain from changing your name, bio, or profile after you have officially put it all together as you do not want to confuse people by having your branding change too frequently.

Changing your branding too frequently prevents people from remembering who you are or having a clear image of what it is that you offer which can interrupt your ability to build relationships with your followers and keep them interested in your content.

Familiarizing Yourself With the Instagram Profile

The Instagram profile has a few different areas that you need to familiarize yourself with when it comes to developing a profile to share with your audience.

Understanding what the purpose and value is with each of these elements will help you see how it all flows together to cultivate your presence, allowing you to begin to devise a plan for how you will have each of these elements working together in perfect harmony.

If you fail to put all of these pieces together into one cohesive image, it can damage your ability to be understood and recognized by your followers, so take the time to understand what each element is and how it connects to the other elements of your profile.

The elements of your Instagram profile include your username, your name, your profile image, your bio, your website, your story highlights, and your image feed.

All seven of these elements are visible as soon as someone lands on your profile without them even having to scroll to view the information or see any more of your profile. If you can capture people's attention with this part of your page, you will have a much easier time getting them to stay on your page, acquaint themselves with your brand, and hopefully start following you.

Your username is important as it defines you against the rest of the Instagram community, and it also serves as a tool for people to find you. Your username will be visible in everything you do, from posting to commenting or otherwise interacting, so you want to make sure you have chosen something that clearly defines who you are and what you have to offer.

Your name should be an extension of your username and, if used properly, should expand on who you are and what you have to offer.

Your name will be seen in certain engagements on Instagram, such as when you view peoples' stories, and they can see who viewed their stories on their own feed. It is also the first thing people will look at on your profile after your profile picture itself, so it needs to be descriptive enough to encourage them to read your bio.

Your profile image is the picture associated with your account, and it will also be visible in everything that you do. Anytime you post, comment on a post, share a story, view a story, or otherwise engage on Instagram, you will have your profile image visible next to your username. This also serves as a first point of contact with your audience, so it should be an image of something that you want to have associated with your brand at all times.

If your profile name, username, and profile image all capture someone's attention, they are going to read your bio.

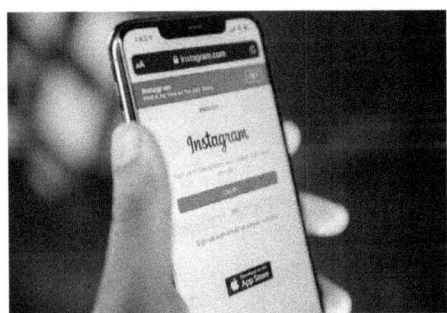

Your bio gives you 150 characters to describe what your personal brand is, and you need to use it effectively. This is the only space you really have to describe "who" and "what." The purpose of this part of your profile is to elaborate on the three initial points of contact while also encouraging people to tap on your images and read your captions, which is where you will get to provide more context for your brand.

Under your bio, you can add a website if you have one — which you should.

You can publish a low-cost website that allows you to give even more insight into who you are and where else you are online, as well as offer more content for your followers. Many influencers use their website to post the occasional blog post as well as to link to their other profiles and build an email list.

Your story highlights are where you can take stories you have made and group the highlights together for followers to see.

Many new followers will want to "binge" your content so that they can see exactly who you are and what you are all about.

You can also leverage these highlights to provide even more insight into your brand, such as through having a highlight for each of your brand "pillars."

Lastly, your image feed is where you are going to be regularly sharing new content with your followers. Aside from your stories, this is where you get to put "consumable" content for your followers, which means you are regularly uploading new content for them to see and interact with.

As far as your profile goes, at a glance, you want the top 3-6 images to all to create an aesthetically appealing image so that when people land on your profile, they feel drawn to scroll down and view more of what you have to offer.

Choosing Your Business Name and Logo

The first three areas of your profile that you need to create include your business name, username, and logo.

Creating the perfect name and logo for your profile ensures that you have the first point of contact established and perfected so that when people come across you, they are likely to click onto your profile.

You need to use a name and image that will entice people and have them wanting to learn more about who you are and what you have to offer.

Creating a name for your business can be somewhat intimidating as you are going to need to use this exact same name across all of your platforms so that people know who you are and can find you anywhere that you might be spending time online.

There are a few ways that you can come up with the perfect name, depending on what you want to build and how you want to be known.

Many influencers will use their own name to create their business, especially if they want to be building a personal brand. With that being said, your name may already be in use online, so you might have to find a unique way to use your name to set you apart from whoever else has your name, too.

The key to setting yourself apart is to refrain from using strange spelling, number sequences, or punctuation to differentiate yourself. These three adaptations can be challenging to remember and, since most people won't remember, can result in you driving a lot of traffic to someone else's pages. Instead, you want to differentiate yourself by including a word next to your own name that coincides with what it is that you have to offer. Some people will use a prefix to their name.

Others will include things like "xo" or their location following their username, such as "@johndoenyc" and others will include an entirely separate word that resonates with their brand, such as "@johndoefitness". If you are building a brand that will be centered around a blog, you might want to pick a name entirely separate from your own, then have yourself known as being the owner behind that brand.

In this sense, you are not necessarily personal branding, but you are still branding yourself and building a brand that is unique to you. Some great examples of using a name other than your own to brand yourself online include "Pretty In Pink," "Lemons and Lipstick," "Pursuing Pretty," "Chats With Coffee," and other similar names that set the tone for who you are and what you talk about.

If you do choose to use a brand name that is different from your own name, try to keep it short, simple, and memorable. People will be more likely to find you and follow you that way.

Once you have chosen your name, you need to set that name as your username and then create your business name on your profile.

Regardless of how you have branded yourself with your username or your brand name, the actual "name" spot on your profile should say your personal name, or whatever name you personally want to be known by. Not having your personal name anywhere on your account can take away from the "personal brand" aspect that influencers need and could make it much harder for you to earn a trusting following.

After your name has been worked out, you need to choose your image. Your image should be reflective of the name you have chosen and should reflect the fact that you are an influencer. Some influencers will use logos in their profile image, although this approach is far more common with businesses that have actual products.

If you are running a blog, however, you may want to use the logo from your blog here to help connect your blog and image together as one unique entity. Otherwise, use a photo of yourself that clearly reflects your brand and helps people recognize who you are.

A clear headshot with elements that are unique to your brand is a great way to associate yourself with your brand while also sending a message about who you are and what your unique aesthetic is.

Creating the Perfect Bio for Your Profile

After your potential follower has been enticed by your initial point of contact, you need to provide more context around who you are through what you share in your bio.

Your bio can only be 150 characters, so you need to be as clear and to the point as you can be in just 1-2 sentences. At this point, the only questions you need to answer are "who?" and "why?" as clearly as possible.

If you answer these two questions well enough, your potential followers will look at your content and gain more context on your brand through your captions.

There are many different ways to approach your bio, although you can easily decide which approach you will take by determining who you are, what audience you want to communicate with, and how you want to communicate with that audience.

Knowing the answer to these questions will help you make important decisions such as what type of information you will place there, how much, and whether or not you will use emojis or other design elements to create your bio.

One great way to get inspiration on how to create your bio is to look at other influencers who are running personal brands similar to the brand you want to develop. While you do not want to copy these other influencers exactly, this can inspire you to create a bio that will resonate with your target audience and reflect your brand accurately.

After you have an idea of how it should look and what you need to say in order to entice your audience, you can start creating your own bio.

It is always a good idea to test out a few bios and compare them to see which one you like the most. You may also find yourself wanting to slightly refine your bio once you know more about your target audience and your marketing strategy.

With that being said, once you have landed on a bio that you like, you need to maintain that bio without changing it, as changing it can confuse your audience and diminish your memorability.

Taking Advantage of Business Profiles

In an effort to improve their accessibility for businesses, Instagram offers business profiles that unlock countless features designed to help you design, promote, and advertise your Instagram business account.

Upgrading to a business account gives you access to all of these features and tailors your Instagram experience to one that is centered around growing and promoting your business on the platform.

As an influencer, you also have the opportunity to tap into another form of upgraded account known as a "creator" account, which is designed specifically for influencers. Again, this account offers features that are unique to your business platform, and that allows you to grow your business more effectively on Instagram.

I strongly advise that you take advantage of one of these upgraded accounts on Instagram if you are going to be running an influencer account or business account, as they will allow you to increase your visibility and maximize your reach on the platform.

With that being said, you will need to decide which one is right for you and your needs based off of what your goals are with running your business on Instagram.

Business accounts give you access to weekly data to show you how your account has been performing
and how much attraction you are gaining off of your presence.

They also allow you to organize your inbox based on messages you want to receive notifications for, messages you want to receive but do not need to be notified for, and messages from people who you are not actively following.

You can also create specific call-to-actions with your business account, including using buttons like "click to call" or "email now!" options. With access to a business account, you also gain the ability to create paid advertisements which allows you to use actual ads to grow your account, which is something many businesses swear by when it comes to increasing their reach.

Creator accounts are designed specifically for influencers and help create a more customized solution for influencers who want to expand on Instagram. Creator accounts actually offer more customized analytics by showing you daily data on audience growth, what specific types of content stimulates growth or losses in your audience, and more.

These more specific analytics ensure that you are able to clearly analyze all of the content you put out and create more of the content that builds your following. With your creator account, you also gain the ability to eliminate the call-to-action from your posts so that if you run your business exclusively on social media, you are not stuck with useless buttons that drive your audience away from your platform.

As well, you gain the upgraded inbox folders and the ability to create paid promotions on Instagram.

Connecting Your Profile to a Facebook Page

When you create a creator account or business account on Instagram, you are going to be prompted to create a Facebook page, too. This is necessary as Instagram will not allow you to transform your account into a business or creator one without connecting it to a Facebook page.

If you do not already have a Facebook page, Instagram will help you create one so that you can upgrade your account as needed.

There are two things you gain from having a Facebook page linked to your Instagram, aside from the fact that you cannot even create a business account without doing this.

The first benefit you gain is that your Instagram page will display your "category" or industry under your name once you have linked the account. So, if you make a Facebook page and set your category to "Public Figure," your Instagram account will say "Public Figure" on it, too. Choose the category that best represents who you are and what you do.

The second thing you gain from linking your Facebook to your Instagram is access to the Facebook ad center, which is where you design ads for Instagram, too. Instagram does not have its own built-in ad platform, so you will need to create all of your ads through the Facebook platform in order to run them on Instagram.

The benefit here is that the Facebook ad manager is advanced and intuitive, meaning it provides you with the ability to create incredibly high-quality ads that can also have high conversion rates.

If you do not plan on using your Facebook page to run your business, consider at least posting 3-5 pieces of unique content on it per week. Or, better yet, share from your Instagram page to your business page.

This way, people who may find you on Facebook realize you are an active account and can find you on Instagram and start following you on the platform where you hang out the most.

you are the writer of your own story. so write something good everyday

Chapter 2

Choosing Your Target Audience

After you have a profile, you are going to want to focus on building followers, as followers are the very people who will engage with your brand and give you an active audience of people to advertise to and convert into buyers.

One big mistake people make when it comes to growing their audience is not being selective about who they are advertising to and, therefore, having an audience that does not entirely resonate with their brand.

While it may seem like a good idea to get as many people following you as possible, the reality is that unengaged followers are not that valuable to your brand *and* they can disrupt your engagement ratios.

The better solution is to identify who your target audience is *first* and then begin to create content to target that audience and grow your followers from that particular category of people. This way, your audience is far more likely to be engaged and connected to you.

Once you create your target audience, you might find that you need to slightly adapt the language in your bio to appeal to your audience better.

Do not be afraid to make these subtle adjustments early on to create a profile that is far more appealing to your audience, but avoid making too many changes.

Stay as clear and to-the-point as possible while still speaking in a way that your audience will understand and appreciate, as well as one that reflects your brand properly.

Creating Your Marketing Goals and Rules

Tapping into the right audience starts with knowing what it is that you actually want to be doing with your business.

Start by setting some goals for yourself that define what you want to be doing, how you want to be marketing, how much you want to earn, and what your non-negotiables are when it comes to running your perfect influencer business.

While you may not know any marketing strategies right now, get an idea of what it is that you want to be doing so that you can identify how you are going to go about doing it.

Since you are planning on running a business on Instagram, it would be a good idea to start by focusing on what you want your income to look like through your brand.

Having an idea of what type of money you want to be earning allows you to consider what type of audience you need to tap into in order to match your income goals.

For example, if you want to earn $3-5,000 per month, you may only need an audience of 5-10,000 people. However, if you want to earn $10,000+ per month, you will want to start focusing on building your audience out to about 100,000+ people.

Knowing the size of the audience you want allows you to later decide what niche will be ideal, as you will be able to narrow down your niche based on how big you can reasonably grow your audience within that particular niche.

After you know how much you want to earn from your business, you need to decide what you want your business to look like.

In other words, how would you want to structure your business in order for it to match your personality and your needs while also reasonably giving you access to the level of income that you want to be earning? How many times would you be posting, what would you be posting about, and what type of interaction or energy levels would be required of you to keep up with your chosen business?

Lastly, consider your personality and really make sure that you are creating a vision that matches who you are.

What are some non-negotiable things that you need to have, or not have, in your business in order for you to continually run it?

If you are going to be personally branding your Instagram account, you need to create a business that you are excited about and that you want to continue showing up for.

If you are not excited or really all that into what you are doing, you are going to have a hard time truly offering any level of commitment and consistency to your brand, which means your chances of failure increase exponentially.

Consider what it is that you like talking about, how you like talking about it, and in what ways you would want to show up to talk about said thing.

Let yourself really focus on creating a vision for your business that allows you to stay excited and engaged with things that you are interested in so that you are more likely to show up, stay committed and consistent, and do your best.

Selecting the Perfect (Profitable) Niche

Now that you have a vision of what you want for your brand, you need to discover the proper niche that is going to allow you to grow into that vision in every way possible.

The ideal niche is one that has a large enough audience that you can create the level of engagement and prosperity that you desire, while also being able to engage with that audience in a way that is enjoyable for you.

As a personal brand, your niche should fit your profit goals as well as your personal goals and personality so that you can enjoy being an active part of that niche and so that you are motivated to become the best of the best in that particular area of your life.

Unlike when it comes to creating your vision, where the first thing you want to do is narrow your focus down by identifying what type of income you want to earn when it comes to choosing your niche you need to consider your passions.

In many cases, having the right level of passion in a tight or slightly smaller niche can actually be more profitable than being engaged in a larger niche that you are not particularly passionate about. With that in mind, consider the top 2-3 things that you are passionate about and decide which of these things you could comfortably talk about for a long time, such as for years on end.

Once you have 2-3 things in mind, start putting those ideas to the test by discovering which of them is strong enough to actually help you create the vision you have for your life and your business. With each of these 2-3 topics on hand, start identifying problems you could solve, or how you could show up in that particular niche to provide something that is not already being provided by someone else, or that maybe isn't being provided well enough by someone else.

For example, maybe you discover that you are passionate about travel, but not enough people are talking about traveling safely as a single person or traveling when you are physically impaired such as with a physical disability.

You want to have a specific focus that is going to be unique to you and that will allow you to stand out from the rest of the niche while still having something interesting and relevant to talk about.

Avoid making your area of focus *too* specific as doing this could result in you having too narrow of an audience to market to, thus eliminating your profitability.

Now that you have a general idea of what you could be doing. Start looking for other people who are doing the same thing. See if you can find any influencers who have the same or similar area of focus and research what they are doing and how they are doing it. This is going to give you two important pieces of information: the realization of what is possible for you, and the ability to identify how you can do better than the people who are already out there doing what you want to be doing.

Lastly, you need to identify the profitability of your niche. Getting involved in a niche that is not profitable or engaged enough is not ideal, as this is going to massively limit your profitability and strip you of your ability to grow your business. There is no point nurturing an audience that is unable to get you the types of results you desire, as long term, this will leave you feeling unfulfilled and as though you have wasted your time and energy on something that was not worth it.

Determining Your Brand's Unique Voice

Now that you have your niche narrowed down, you need to start identifying what your brand "personality" is and how you are going to show up in order to communicate with that niche. As you launch your personal brand, you may think that your personality is exactly perfect for your niche and that by just being you, you are doing your business a favor, and you are going to create success.

While authenticity is important, you also want to make sure that you are speaking in a way that is relatable and receivable by your niche audience.

For this reason, you need to create a unique brand voice that you will use to communicate with your audience.

Creating your brand's unique voice starts with understanding who it is that you are serving, what niche you are a part of, and how you want people to view you. You will be creating your entire reputation around what you say and how you say it, so you need to be highly intentional about creating your brand's voice.

After you have nailed down "who" your brand is going to be, you need to start creating rules around what you will and will not say as a part of your brand.

Having these rules in place will allow you to be authentic without sharing parts of your personality or thoughts that may be irrelevant to your niche.

It is important that you adhere to these rules once you have made them, as you want to maintain a consistent message and personality for your audience to follow.

If you find yourself straying away or sharing off-topic messages, you are likely to lose your following while also possibly losing out on brand deals because you have strayed away from your branded personality.

When you create your brand voice, you should start by choosing three describing words that will define what you say and how you say it.

These three words should be relevant to your personal brand, authentic to you, and relevant to your audience so that they resonate with what you are saying and continue to follow you.

The words should also work together to describe a similar image, as having conflicting descriptions could lead to you having a confusing and chaotic brand. For example, you may want to describe your voice as being "friendly, kind, and welcoming" which would all work together effectively. However, if you tried to have a brand that was "friendly, welcoming, and abrasive," that would not work well together as you would be contradicting yourself and, therefore, struggling to create a consistent image.

To choose your unique voice, take a look at your competitors and see what their voice is like.

Try to summarize your competitors' voices in three words each and see what similar personality traits arise between each of your competitors.

Get an idea of how these personality traits relate to your audience and how they relate to you and your brand, as well.

Then, take a look at how you could relate to your brand and start to define your three describing words, based on who you are and how you naturally talk, as well as how you feel your audience would like to be talked to.

After you have defined your three descriptive words for your voice, you need to make your rules around how you are going to talk to your audience.

This includes rules such as what tone you are going to use, what types of language you will use, and how you will communicate with your audience.

Some rules you might have could be: no cussing, keeping jokes to a minimum, being fact-based and well-educated in your information, or otherwise.

Be aware when choosing rules for your messaging, as some brands may not want to work with influencers who regularly cuss or who are consistently sharing information that contradicts their values.

Be mindful of your choice of language so that you can speak in a way that increases your potential to receive brand deals while maintaining your image, too.

Deciding on What Types of Content to Post

Instagram offers many unique ways that you can post content for your audience, and you are going to decide which ways you are going to take advantage of.

The content types you can create for Instagram includes posts with captions, stories, live videos, and IGTV videos.

You are going to want to decide which of these types of content you want to make the most and how you are going to make this content so that you can create a coherent brand that flows well together while also providing your audience with plenty of great content.

Posts with captions are the bread and butter of Instagram, so you will need to make sure that you are posting those on a regular basis.

Ideally, you should be posting around 1-3 times per day, depending on what your marketing strategy is. As you post this content, you will need to decide whether you want to become known for longer captions or shorter captions, as well as what type of content you are going to put in the captions.

Are you going to ask questions? Are you going to offer knowledge or insightful guidance to your audience? How are you going to use captions and images to build a relationship with your audience?

Stories are another essential on Instagram, as many Instagram users now go to the app just to click through stories. In fact, some people barely scroll the feed anymore but instead just watch the stories of their favorite people to follow.

You can create stories by sharing videos and images of your day with your audience, particularly the parts that are relevant to your brand, or you can create graphic art images using apps like Canva and StoryArt to create unique story experiences.

Ideally, you should upload between 10-40 stories per day as an influencer, as this allows you to create plenty of binge-worthy content for your audience.

Don't forget to put some of your stories into a highlight reel on your page so that new followers can be introduced to your older content!

Live videos appear where stories are, and they are a way for you to interact with your audience in real-time. Not all brands use live videos; however, live videos can be incredibly useful as they allow you to directly communicate with your live audience and give a more personalized experience for your followers.

Often, influencers will use live videos to share open conversations with their audience about whatever their audience wants to talk about which serves as a way to build a more meaningful relationship with your audience.

Some users will also use live videos to share content live and answer questions immediately, or to share live interviews or conversations with fellow Instagram influencers so that their audience can learn through that interview or conversation.

IGTV is similar to YouTube, except that your videos are shown in the portrait mode instead of landscape mode on your phone. Many influencers use IGTV videos to share tutorials, information, Q&A videos, or other similar information- or entertainment-based videos with their followers.

While it is not necessary to use IGTV, it is recommended that you use it once in a while as studies show that more than 70% of mobile users enjoy consuming video content, and many of those individuals prefer it over reading captions on posts.

As well, if you create an IGTV video, you can link it to your main page as a post, meaning you will be populating your feed with new posts each time you upload new video content.

Many creators use IGTV instead of regular posts thanks to this new feature.

When it comes to building your brand, you need to decide what type of content is going to be the most relevant for your audience, as well as what type of content you are going to be most willing to make.

You do not want to commit to making content that you absolutely do not enjoy making, or that you struggle to make on a regular basis, as this will result in you not keeping up with your consistency.

To start, pick 2 ways that you will interact with your audience on a daily basis and then grow your platform out from there.

Creating a Strong Content Calendar

A content calendar is an important tool that influencers use to make sure that they are producing and uploading new content on a consistent basis.

Consistency is the key to growing an influencer business, so you are going to need to keep yourself consistent and focused if you want to grow your personal brand on Instagram.

Using a content calendar, you can stay focused on what type of content needs to be uploaded when, as well as what type of focus you want to take on. Many times, influencers want to build their themes around upcoming holidays and events that are relevant to their audience so they use a content calendar to keep track of these holidays and events, effectively allowing them to plan out their themes.

Early on, I suggest you start by creating a content calendar that focuses no more than one month into the future.

At this point, you are new to posting, so it is difficult for you to know what strategies are going to work and what strategies are not going to work, so you will want to use a month-to-month approach to test new things out.

As you continue to test out new strategies, you can begin to create your content calendars further out into the future since you will have more reliable information at this point.

Refining Your Approach to Posting

As you continue to build out your new content calendars, it is important that you continually refine your approach to posting.

Refining your approach allows you to recognize what types of strategies are working so that you can continue using them, while also recognizing what types of strategies are not working so that you can stop using them.

Ideally, you should only refine your approach every 3 months unless you can guarantee that a strategy you are using is absolutely not working, or is turning people away.

Switching your strategies too frequently can result in you actually destroying your consistency and damaging your growth, rather than serving it.

When it does come time to refine your posting approach, you want to look for three specific pieces of information: what types of content are most (and least) popular, what styles of content are most (and least) popular, and what time of day are you getting the most engagement?

Pay attention to what type of content your audience likes consuming the most.

Do they like videos or posts? Are they reading your longer captions, or do they prefer shorter ones? In your stories, are they engaging with you? Do they prefer picture-based stories or video-based stories? Are they enjoying your IGTV content? Do they answer your questions?

Get clear on what specific types of content your audience likes the most so that you can create more of these types of content.

You should also pay attention to what styles of content your audience likes consuming the most.

By this, I mean, are they enjoying your entertaining content or your educational content the most? Are you attracting a bigger audience through speaking in a kinder tone, or a more humorous tone? Does your audience prefer stories or cold-hard facts?

Get clear on what writing and speaking styles they prefer so that you can speak to them in the way they prefer to be spoken to, which will effectively help you gain the results you desire.

Lastly, pay attention to when your audience is the most active. Ideally, you should be posting content when your audience is the most active so that you can expect increased engagement rates from your audience.

Another great engagement tip is to comment on your followers' posts immediately after posting a new piece of content so that they are more likely to actually see the new content that you posted.

"Be the CHANGE that you wish to see in the world."

MAHATMA GANDHI

Chapter 3

Creating Your Narrative

While you have already put a great deal of effort into building out your brands' voice and outlining the skeleton for your posting strategies, it is time for you to go deeper and really hammer out your perfect influencer vision.

You need to get clear on what your narrative is and practice sharing that narrative in every way possible when it comes to creating branded content.

Your images, videos, and written language should all be sharing the same story so that your audience can immediately identify who you are, what your story is, and why they need to start listening to your story.

Story branding was actually discovered and put into action long before Instagram came around, but the platform itself relies heavily on story branding due to its nature of sharing images and captions with your audience.

Knowing what your story is and how to convey it to your audience ensures that you will be leveraging the platform in the best ways possible, ultimately allowing you to master the platform and explode your following.

If you can really get the hang of story branding, you will be far more likely to gain a strong, engaged following and transform that following into an active audience that purchases from you and supports your brand in every way possible.

Instagram Is for Story Branding

Instagram was built for story branding. The constant stream of images and video-based content provides the perfect platform to share your stories through visual, written, and audible stories that you create specifically for your audience.

Knowing how to take advantage of each of these elements and put it together to create the story of your brand means you have the capacity to leverage each element of Instagram and turn it into your own work of art.

The best part is, you do not actually need to be an artist to grow your brand on Instagram, you simply need to be willing to have a strong strategy and the ability to recreate what works (while letting go of what doesn't.)

On Instagram, your profile is where you get to tell the bulk of your story.

Your username, name, profile image, bio, and website all read as the "summary" of your story, much like the backside of a novel you might pick up in a bookstore. Through your feed of images, you provide the story itself.

This part of the story is often slow-building, though it is consistent and regularly gives you the opportunity to provide large elements of the plot to your audience. Through a few well-written sentences or even a couple of short paragraphs, you give your audience the story they desire to read more of.

The images you pair the captions with additional context and depth to the story, making it that much more intriguing for your audience.

On some profiles, the pictures *are* the story and the captions remain small and intentional, and for the audiences of those unique influencers, this approach works perfectly.

This is a great testament to the fact that you truly do have a lot of creative freedom when it comes to building your personal brand on Instagram.

Your stories offer you the opportunity to provide an even deeper context for your audience.

If the feed is where you tell the story, then your stories are where you get to offer behind the scenes insight to content that did not make it to the main story, as well as to the character who plays the main role in the story.

Here, you get to build a more personalized relationship with your audience, offering them a deeper connection with you as a person and an influencer.

Your live videos allow you to go from sharing your behind the scenes content to completely breaking the barrier between you and your audience and communicating with them directly, live.

If you use them correctly, these videos help you build meaningful relationships with your audience that allows your audience to become far more invested in who you are and what it is that you have to offer.

This is where they get to go from being your followers to being your devoted fans.

Lastly, IGTV is a great opportunity to build your main story while also providing the element of personal connection through voice and eye contact. Looking at the camera and speaking candidly is a great opportunity to allow your followers to feel as though you are communicating with them directly, which is said to greatly enhance the relationship between your brand and your followers.

Creating a Flow of High-Quality Images

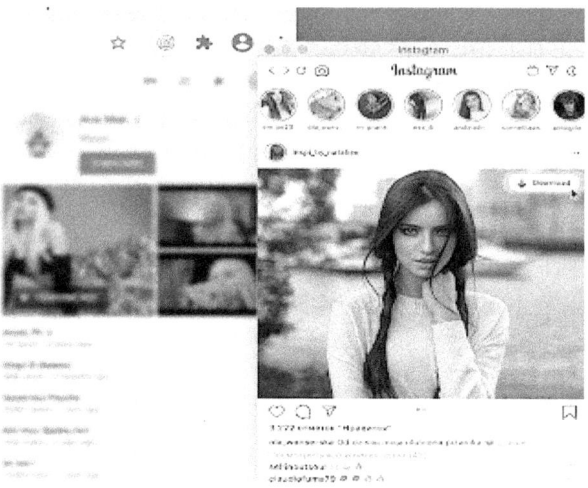

It's true what they say. A picture really does say a thousand words. On Instagram, using high-quality images gives you the opportunity to create captivating content that tells a story to your audience.

Ideally, your pictures should be strong enough to tell a story all on their own, even if the person viewing your profile were to never actually click onto one of your posts and read the captions.

Having strong images that tell your story on their own ensures that you are painting a picture that is interesting and worth looking deeper into for people who land on your profile.

If you do this part properly, people will find your content, become interested in your story, and feel compelled to explore deeper and read further into what it is that you are sharing with them.

Creating a stream of high-quality images that tells a story requires a strong strategy that will allow you to clearly understand what your own story is so that your images can convey that story for you, too.

It will also take some practice, as you are going to need to get used to creating an image-based story that looks good on its own, as well as one that looks good when it is combined with the other images on your profile.

There are truly countless ways that you can provide an image-based story for your followers, so the best way to narrow down what strategy you are going to use is to identify what story it is that you are trying to tell.

Your story will be the combination of your niche, your voice, and your unique personality. Combined, you will have a cohesive story that allows you to convey your message to your audience before they ever even stop to look at what you have written.

Strategizing your image-based story can be done effortlessly through first choosing a color scheme.

A color scheme ensures that your images all look good on their own, while also looking good together.

Ideally, your color scheme should match the tone and voice of your brand, as this contributes to you having a coherent brand that is enjoyable to look at and easy to understand.

After you have your color scheme, you need to choose five elements that are going to be relevant to your story. Choosing five elements that complement the rest of your brand will give you the opportunity to create a coherent story that easily works together with the rest of your branding elements to create a unique follower experience.

These five elements could be anything such as your dog, music, yoga, your friends, your family, pineapples, a certain texture, or anything else that is relevant to your brand.

Once you have these five elements decided, every single image you share should have one of the five elements.

At least three of those five elements should be shared on a continuous basis to make a consistent story that is still dynamic enough to be enjoyable.

Improving Your Photography Skills

Since Instagram is all about visual content, knowing how to take killer images is essential in building the best Instagram page possible.

While you certainly do not need to be an expert photographer to make your profile enjoyable, you should have at least a few tips under your belt to help you capture images that are far more appealing and enjoyable for your audience to browse.

The following nine steps will help you start taking better images for your feed so that you can have a page that is worthy of being followed.

The first step is to get your lighting proper. Natural light is the best light for Instagram as it creates more natural-looking photographs that are brighter and richer in color.

Avoid using flash whenever possible, as flash will flatten the photo and wash out your subject, making the image less appealing.

The second step in improving your pictures is to avoid overexposing your images. While lighter and brighter images are trending on Instagram, using overexposed images is not ideal as it ruins the quality of your image, and it cannot be fixed using any editing tools. You are better off to take slightly darker photographs and lighten them with a photo editing tool.

The third step is to shoot at the right time. Golden Hour, which is a time of day where the sun is low over the horizon, is a natural "filter" you can use to improve the quality of your photographs.

Taking photos during golden hour, or on an overcast day, ensures that you are able to capture great images that are not too bright or overpowering.

The fourth step is to follow the rule of thirds. Imagine your camera has a 3x3 grid on it (or turn the grid setting on if this is an option on your camera) and align subjects of your photograph along the grid lines to create balance.

You can center your subject, or set it off to one of the two sides along the gridline to make a beautiful photograph.

The fifth step is to consider where you are taking your photographs from.

The average person will hold their phone up around their eye level and take a picture exactly as they see things in that moment.

- How could you change your viewpoint to offer a more unique viewing experience, though?
- Could you get lower and look up, or get higher and look down?
- Could you try a new vantage point?

Look for a fresh perspective that is unique from what the average person is showing and offer your images from that point of view.

The sixth step in taking better photographs is framing your subject. Leaving space around the focal point of your photo, space that photographers call *negative space,* can help add more visual interest to what you are taking an image of.

Negative space helps create more texture in your photograph, ultimately helping make it far more enjoyable to view.

Drawing your viewer's eye is actually step number seven, too. In photography, there are elements called "leading lines" that run through your image and can draw your viewers' attention to a specific point.

For example, the line of a horizon, the line on the side of a building, or even the line of a certain focal point you have all draws lines across your photograph.

Use these lines to draw your viewers' attention to the focal point by lining them up as if they lead you toward that point like a map for your attention.

The eighth step of taking better photographs is to add better depth.

Many new photographers will focus solely on the subject of their photo, but this can actually take away from the quality of that photo by not adding enough dynamic and dimension into it. Rather than getting too focused on just the subject, see if you can line that subject up in a spot that has a significant amount of depth and texture to it, while still maintaining negative space in your photograph.

For example, rather than taking a photograph of yourself against a blank wall, take a photo of yourself in a park or surrounded by something that is naturally interesting, as this will enhance the quality of your photograph.

The ninth and final step is to get creative with your images. Instagram is full of trends, but trends can lose their appeal rather quickly, and they can also lead to users having accounts full of images that are so similar that they are almost not worth looking at.

Rather than having yourself caught up in trends and losing out on your individuality, be unique and be creative with your photographs.

Take photographs that represent your brand and what you care about, not just images that reflect what is currently trending on Instagram.

Recording the Perfect Insta-Worthy Videos

In the past, Instagram was primarily built around photographs. However, as the platform has grown, they have added a lot of opportunities for users to engage through video content, too.

Stories, live videos, IGTV, and inline videos right there in your feed are all ways for you to share video content with your followers. It is highly recommended that you take advantage of sharing video, too, because statistics show that about 70% of Instagram users are watching video content.

That is way too big of an audience to miss out on, so don't forget to create video-based content, too!

Part of creating video content is knowing how to create content that is actually going to get viewed.

On stories, this can include short 5-120 second video clips of what you are experiencing in your daily life or tips you want to share directly with your audience through your stories. On live video, IGTV, and inline video, this should be content that is going to be worthy of being viewed again and again.

Usually, this content either needs to be educational or entertaining in order for your viewer to actually watch it, which means how-to videos, tutorials, tips, hack videos, and videos that make you laugh, cry, or otherwise feel something inside are all great for Instagram.

Creating better Instagram video content is just as important as creating better Instagram photographic content. The increasing number of viewers also means an increasing number of people making video content, which means, to put it simply: if you are not creating great content, people are going to go elsewhere.

On the one hand, if your content is educational or entertaining enough, people will likely put up with a certain amount of low-quality video elements while they watch your content. However, if the payoff is not enough *or* the video quality is really bad, people are unlikely to watch what you are creating.

To create better video content for Instagram, there are four steps you need to take in order to make sure your content is perfect. These steps include having clear goals, telling a story, lighting your video, and shooting your video.

If you are using a short inline video, you are only going to have 60 seconds worth of content to share. If you are using IGTV, you can share up to 10 minutes of video content. You need to decide what it is that you want to share and then create a clear goal for that which can be met within either 60 seconds or 10 minutes.

Your goal could be anything from trying to get new followers to trying to gain more engagement with the followers you already have or even driving more traffic to your website. Whatever your goal is, have it clearly defined before you even begin to plan and shoot the video.

Videos should always be based around telling a story. While you don't need to make a professional storyboard to tell your story, you should have a clear story that you want to share that aligns with your goals and supports your followers with helping you fulfill your goals.

Ideally, you should divide your story into three parts: beginning, middle, and end. You should also clarify how long you want each segment of your video to last *before* you start filming it. Make sure your end ends with a call to action so that your viewers can help you fulfill your goal, too.

The best way to light your video is to go outside and use natural light or to film near the window during a time of day where the light is not directly beaming in through your window.

Never shoot under overhead lights because these tend to create strange visual effects and can cast odd shadows over your entire video. Do not be afraid to move around in order to find the best lighting to film in, as an attractive video will be far more likely to keep peoples' attention.

Lastly, you need to. On the one hand shoot your video. For starters, shoot your video in portrait mode as this ensures that your content can be shared on IGTV, too. Even if you are creating it for inline video content, adding it to your IGTV will likely increase viewership and help you get even closer to reaching your goal with that content.

Then, you need to make sure that you keep the shot entirely focused on your subject the entire time.

Do not let the subject go out of focus as this can be distracting and can completely destroy the quality of your video. And, of course, keep the shot steady. Do not shake your hands around or use a surface that results in your camera shaking around.

Try using a small tripod for your phone so that your device stays steady and gets a nice, clean shot.

When to Use Sponsored Posts

Sponsored posts are often the goal for most influencers, as these are the posts you are paid to put on your account and share with your followers.

With that being said, there are some general guidelines that influencers should follow to ensure that they are getting the best quality content out for their followers and that their followers continue to remain engaged even after they start doing sponsored posts.

First and foremost, sponsored posts should never be the *only* thing you post on Instagram. Your followers have come to you because they like you, and they trust you and, to be honest, it is tacky to sell to them in every single post. The general rule of thumb is to provide 80% value and 20% sales posts.

This means for every 5 posts, 1 should be organic and 1 should be sponsored. If you want to do more sponsored posts, focus on creating more organic content, too. On Instagram, this can be varied slightly as you may reserve your feed for more selective photos, in which case it is okay to do a higher value/sponsor ratio, as long as you are using features like your stories to provide non-sponsored content on a regular basis.

The key here is to make sure that your audience never feels like you only show up to sell to them, as they will start to feel as though you are inauthentic and will question the trust they have built-in you.

As long as you use the proper value/sponsor ratio, you can continue to do sponsored posts as often as you want. As with your personal posts, you want to make sure your sponsored posts are all high value and that the images or videos are captured in high quality and enjoyable to look at or watch.

You should also make sure that you are completely transparent in every sponsored post you make, as this is an important way to maintain trust with your audience.

Furthermore, admitting when things are advertisements is actually a requirement of Instagram and uploading a sponsored post without a clear indication that what you have posted is an ad that can result in you having your account suspended.

Lastly, make sure that you only ever do sponsorships with brands that you truly believe in and that you would happily use yourself.

Doing sponsorships with brands you do not believe in or do not like, or brands you have not tried can result in you promoting low-quality companies and could massively destroy your trust between you and your followers.

As well, never sign a deal with a sponsor that disrupts your integrity as you never want to be contractually obligated to lie to your audience or say something out of character.

Partnering With Instagram Influencers and Brands

Partnerships between Instagram influencers and brands are one of the biggest reasons why businesses even exist on Instagram in the first place.

This is the number one way for promoting content through Instagram and, if done right, can earn massive money for both the influencer and the brand. When it comes to being an influencer on Instagram, it is important to realize that brands are not always going to reach out to you and request you to be their influencer.

While some brands might, you are ultimately going to have to put in a lot of work to connect with other influencers and brands to really get your name out there and increase your visibility, as well as increase your success as an influencer.

When it comes to other influencers, connecting with them and doing collaborations is a great way to increase your visibility.

Ideally, you should create honest and authentic relationships with the influencers that you like so that these relationships truly are valuable and enjoyable.

Never connect with another influencer just to get something out of them as your intentions will always become visible at one point or another, and it looks tacky.

Take your time and build genuine relationships with other followers and, if the opportunity eventually arises, you can plan to create collaborations with other influencers.

Collaborations can come in the form of collaborated giveaways, tutorials, entertainment videos, or anything else that you might have available for your audience.

Sometimes, influencers will even collaborate on a brand sponsorship to offer even more value to the brand they are mutually representing. Get creative, and do not be afraid to look for ways for both of you to benefit from your relationship.

Creating relationships with brands is important, too. As you grow, you will begin to understand your audience better, and this means that you will start to understand what types of products they are likely going to enjoy using in their own lives.

Having relationships with brands who fit these descriptions means you can try their products and, if you think your audience will like those products, you can approach brands for potential sponsorship deals. In many cases, brands will happily work with an influencer who can prove that they have the capacity to increase revenue for that brand in a meaningful way. If you get turned down on a deal, do not be afraid to make it known that you would be open to collaborating later on, should that brand change their mind.

Of course, make sure that you are always respectful and grateful when talking to brands no matter what they say as brands will always be far more likely to collaborate with respectful influencers over those who lack respect and kindness toward the people they are working with.

As you continue to build relationships with both influencers and brands, make sure you stay consistent in connecting with them online.

Do not show up, ask for something, and then disappear as this will make you look flaky and will come across as though you were just looking for a deal. Instead, continue nurturing that relationship so that you stay in the foreground and continue to build your presence.

Over time, trust will be built and you will likely be able to mutually enjoy even more perks from that relationship.

Everything You Need to Know About Hashtags

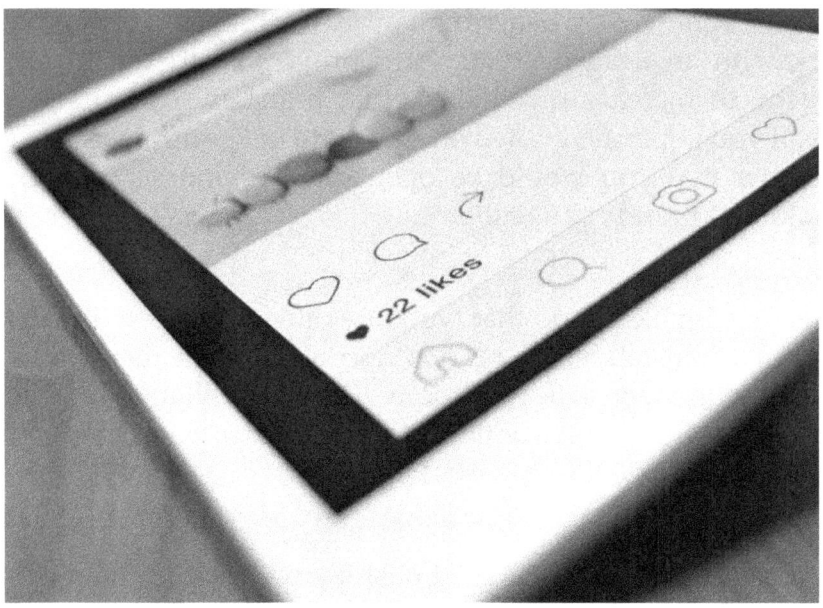

Hashtags are the heart and soul of Instagram. Well, not quite as much as the actual visual content itself, but without effective use of hashtags, it is incredibly challenging to grow your account since no one will be able to find you.

On Instagram, hashtags are used on photographs and these hashtags essentially put those photographs into public "albums," as long as your privacy settings are set to "public" (which they should be.)

These albums are then viewed by people who are interested in them and, if they like your photograph, they will click on it and interact with it.

This is how you attract new viewers to your page and increase your engagement and following. If you fail to use hashtags, you will struggle to get any sort of traction and, as a result, you will not have consistent growth on your profile.

The key to using hashtags is to use them effectively to ensure that you are getting viewed by the right people who are most likely to enjoy your photographs or videos and then actually engage in your content.

You want to use targeted hashtags that are going to help you connect with your target audience effortlessly so that you grow your page and attract new followers on a continuous basis.

This continuous growth, then, attracts even more success to your brand and increases your perceived value when it comes to working with sponsorship deals.

When it comes to using hashtags, there are three things you need to do: research the best ones for your account, use the best ones for your unique photograph, and engage on those hashtags, so you get found.

These three tools are going to massively increase your engagement over time; therefore, drastically increasing your success as an influencer.

You must find and use the right hashtags for your account, and in this day and age, it is imperative that you are not using generic hashtags. Hashtags like "#wellness," "#fitness," "#beauty," "#foodie," and so forth are so overused that at this point, if you use them, your photo is going to get buried rapidly under all of the other users that are adding those hashtags. Repeated use of these hashtags wastes your time as getting buried too quickly means no one is actually going to see what you have posted. Instead, you want to use targeted hashtags that have between 75,000 and 750,000 uses so far.

These hashtags are a great size because they are big enough to prove that they are used often, and they are small enough to avoid you getting buried under new content too quickly.

One great way to start researching new hashtags is to type in a more niche hashtag on your Instagram app and look at related hashtags that come up under it. For example, you might use "#yoganyc" which would bring up related hashtags like "#yogaforeverybody", "#feeltheyogahigh", and "#backbends". These similar hashtags are each niche hashtags that will offer you a more target audience, so you should keep track of them on a note in your phone.

Anytime you go to post a photograph on your Instagram, draw from your note of hashtags for the best hashtags to use. Make sure that every hashtag is relevant to your audience *and* your photo so that you are targeting your audience with content that is relevant to what they are actually looking for.

On Instagram, you can use up to 30 hashtags per picture, so you should use at least 15 or up to 30 hashtags per photograph to make sure you are getting seen by as many people as possible.

Once you have posted your photograph, you should go through at least 3 of those hashtags and comment on five photographs per hashtag with a genuine comment.

This means you should have created 15 comments in total using comments that are more meaningful and genuine than a bunch of emojis or a simple, single-word response.

Be thoughtful in your responses and genuinely engage with other people, as this attracts genuine engagement back to you, too.

You should aim to do this within 30 minutes of posting your own content, as this has been shown to increase engagement based on the current structure of the Instagram algorithm.

DON'T STOP UNTIL YOU'RE PROUD

Chapter 4:

Instagram Stories

Instagram stories were introduced in August of 2016, and they have massively grown in popularity over the past few years. This feature allows users to offer personal, behind-the-scenes type images for their audience so that they can deepen their relationships with their audience and enjoy the perks of having even more connection with their followers.

For influencers, this means you can increase the amount of trust your followers have in you, while also increasing their level of loyalty to you which, ultimately, increases their willingness to buy from you anytime you promote something.

Learning how to use stories properly is an important way to make sure that you are creating stories that your followers will actually enjoy. If you can create engaging stories, your followers will look forward to seeing you in their feed every morning and will feel as though they are genuinely catching up with an old friend. This is the ultimate way to create a positive and meaningful relationship with your followers that will result in you becoming an influncer.

What Is the Value of Instagram Stories?

Instagram stories are a short-lived feature that can only be viewed on your page for 24 hours unless you have placed those stories in a highlighted folder on your main page.

Using Instagram stories is a great way to deliver tons of new content to your audience without bombarding them.

Uploading too much content on your personal feed every day can be overwhelming and, depending on the type of account you have, most experts agree that you should not post any more than 1-3 photos or videos per day. However, you can post up to 99 stories per day without bombarding your followers' feed. With that being said, 99 stories is a lot so you are likely going to want to go with around 10-30 per day.

This way, you are uploading plenty of great content for your followers to engage with, without creating so much content that they get bored and click away from you to view someone else's stories.

Stories give you a chance to get creative in a new way, offer a behind-the-scenes experience for your viewers, and interact with your audience in a unique way.

These days, stories feature questions, polls, and other interactive features that allow you to engage even more with your audience in this unique manner.

You can also doodle on your pictures, add emojis or texts to them, or add unique stickers to your images or videos to make them more enjoyable.

They really are an interactive and enjoyable way to connect with your audience.

As you create story content for your audience, think about fulfilling three needs for every single post: interesting, relevant, and personal. Interesting content ensures that your audience's attention will be captured long enough for them to actually stop and look at what you have posted on your story feed, which means they are more likely to engage with it.

Relevant content means that you are going to be sharing behind the scenes content that they are actually going to care about or relate to so that they are more likely to continue watching.

Personal content means that you are offering content that is "private" so that your followers feel like they are sharing more intimate moments with you in your life. The truth is, people are nosy, and they love to know stuff about other people, and while you do not want to (or need to) give everything away, satisfying their curiosity about who you are outside of your Instagram pictures is a great way to connect even more.

Below, I am going to highlight three big industries on Instagram and give an example of what types of content you could share in your stories if you were in those industries to match all three of these needs.

If you do so, you will exponentially deepen the relationship between you and your audience and, therefore, increase their loyalty and likely to continue following you for years to come.

- **Wellness:** If you run a fitness page, you could share story content such as your personal workout routine, tips you personally use to work out better, your meal plan, food prep tips for eating healthier, advice on what to look for when purchasing fitness equipment or memberships, stories of you shopping for new workout clothes, reviews of workout clothes or equipment you have, and other similar content.

- **Beauty:** If you are sharing makeup looks on your Instagram page, you could share story content such as your skincare routine, honest reviews of makeup, behind the scenes looks of you making content or new looks, pictures of your day-to-day looks, pictures of your makeup station, images of other peoples' looks, wellness tips that contribute to skin health, and other similar content.

- **Food:** If you are sharing food on Instagram, you could share story content such as trips through your local grocery store, shares from restaurants you want to try eating at, stories of you preparing your food, samples of meal plans, advice for shopping for food, meal planning and preparation tips, and other similar content.

Whenever you share content, it should always be about your personal journey, your personal opinion, and your experiences.

Your stories should be as personal to you as possible as people are watching them to get into your life and learn more about you.

With that being said, you do still want to keep your stories relevant as people are not always going to be interested in seeing other areas of your life on your page.

While you can certainly talk about other areas of your life in your stories, such as your dog, your relationship, your work, your studies, and other such things, you should always make sure that these are mixed in with relevant content.

This way, people get to see more of who you are and understand more of what you do while also getting the opportunity to see your "extra" tips and secrets about the topic they actually follow you for.

Engaging With Your Audience Through Stories

There are many ways to engage with your audience through your stories, and it seems like, with every update, Instagram pushes even more ways to engage with your audience through your story feed.

With that being said, there are six ways that you can massively increase engagement through your stories so that you can get even further with them.

The first thing you should do is try telling a story. You can either do this with a few images and some captions over them, or with a short video that you upload to your story feed that contains a beginning, middle, and end. People love listening to stories, especially "extra" stories that are behind-the-scenes in your life.

You should also add captions in your stories, especially when you are creating video content. Some users will simply say "sound on" whereas others will write captions that are similar to what they have said.

Taking a moment to write what you said in a caption means that people who are not able to listen to your content can read what you have written, which is a great way to increase your ability to gain engagement through stories.

Stickers are another great way to increase engagement. Instagram is loaded with images, so taking a moment to make your images unique using interactive stickers that add depth and character to your photographs is a great opportunity to make your stories even more interactive.

You can either use stickers of actual objects, or the stickers that have interactive features such as questions or polls so that viewers can engage directly with the story itself.

Prompts are another great way to engage with your audience. Three prompts that have been known to increase engagement include "hold to read" which prompts the viewer to hold the screen and read what you have shared, "tap for more," which encourages them to view all of the images you have shared, and "get ready to" which builds excitement through your story feed.

Some brands also use "screenshotable" stories, which are stories that viewers can screenshot and then add to their own stories.

If you do this, make them yourself and add your username to them so that if your viewer shares the story to their own stories, their viewers can find you, too.

Screenshotable stories can be of lists, "this or that" type quizzes, or anything else that your viewers can upload and share some information on to personalize it for their own viewers. It could also be wallpapers that your viewer could use for a background on their phone.

Lastly, do not be afraid to directly ask your users for engagement. Upload something interesting and then say "DM for download" to get viewers to DM you for a download link. Ask a question and ask viewers to DM you to answer that question. Share your new post to your story with a "new post" sticker over it and ask viewers to go look at it and read what you have to say. The more you ask for engagement, the more people are likely going to respond and actually do what you have asked. Never underestimate the power of being direct!

Using Text, Hashtags, and Username Tags

You can use text, hashtags, and username tags in your stories as a way to increase engagement and viewership. As you already know, text in the form of prompts or captions is a great way to get your followers to pay attention to what you have posted in your stories.

However, you can also use hashtags and username tags to increase viewership and get your reach extended even further.

Hashtags can be added to your stories simply by adding them in a text box and then clicking the hashtag prompt that comes up at the bottom of the screen.

Doing so ensures that the hashtag has been properly tagged in the story and that your photo is going to appear in the stories associated with that particular hashtag.

You can either openly use hashtags or, as some users do, you can use a hashtag and then make it incredibly tiny and color it to an element in your photo to "hide" it in there. This way, the hashtag exists but no one can see it because it has been hidden within the photograph itself.

Username tags can be used as a way to tag brands, fellow influencers, or people who inspired your story share.

Never tag randomly as this looks spammy and will prevent people from paying attention to you and could leave other notable people in your industry, thinking that you are not ideal for them to collaborate with.

However, tagging relevant brands or accounts in your posts is a great way to increase viewership and maximize engagement.

Some users will even reshare your stories, meaning you will be viewed by their users, too, which is a great way to increase your reach and become even more popular on Instagram.

Leveraging the Story Highlight Feature

Story highlights are select stories that you have chosen to display on your page indefinitely. If you create a story highlight, it will be visible on your page under your bio and above your images, showing people what type of content you have available for them to binge.

Many influencers and brands will use story highlights as a way to create relevant "albums" of stories for their viewers to watch so that their new followers can binge this content and immediately start to feel more connected to the sharer.

You could also use this area to share relevant tips, guidance, advice, or other educational shares so that people can go back to your page to review that content again and again.

For example, if you are a fitness coach, you might share 4-5 simple exercises in a highlight so that new followers can follow those simple exercises and start to get a feel for how you coach them.

No matter who you are or what you share, you should always take advantage of the story highlight feature.

The key to highlights is to make sure that they are relevant to your brand and your account, and that your followers are likely going to see them as being valuable.

They may be somewhat unique from your core message, as long as they are clearly relevant to your overall brand. For example, if you are a beauty influencer who likes to travel a lot, you may have highlights that feature your travels, which is not necessarily beauty-related but it is relevant to your brand.

To make these stories and highlights even more relevant, you might share stories of your unique makeup looks or beauty tips from your different travels so that you are sharing content for both benefits at once.

Story highlights can either be created with images directly out of the story as your highlight cover or with unique covers that you make for the story itself.

Many users will create custom graphics for the story highlight cover using an app like StoryArt or Canva, both of which will let you brand the covers. These branded covers can add to the general aesthetic of your account by keeping everything unique and relevant, as well as organized into your color scheme.

Creating Live Video Content

Live videos are shared into your story feed, and, like your stories, they disappear after 24 hours. Live videos should be used as a way to engage directly with your audience in a highly interactive manner.

When you go live, your audience is going to feel like they are right there with you because they are able to have you read their comments in real-time, which makes it feel like you are speaking directly to them. Many influencers will share live experiences such as a few minutes of a concert or event they are at that is relevant to their brand, as this is a great way to make it feel like your audience is coming along with you.

You can also share live content in the form of Q&As or live conversations with your audience, where you go on with the core purpose of talking to anyone who comments on your feed.

This is common for people who have large, engaged followings as they are more likely to get engagement on their live videos.

Until you have a larger following, consider starting your live videos with a clear goal and then moving into a Q&A style video once you consistently get large enough engagement on your videos to warrant it.

When you love what you have, you have everything you need.

Chapter 5

Business Strategies: From Followers to Customers

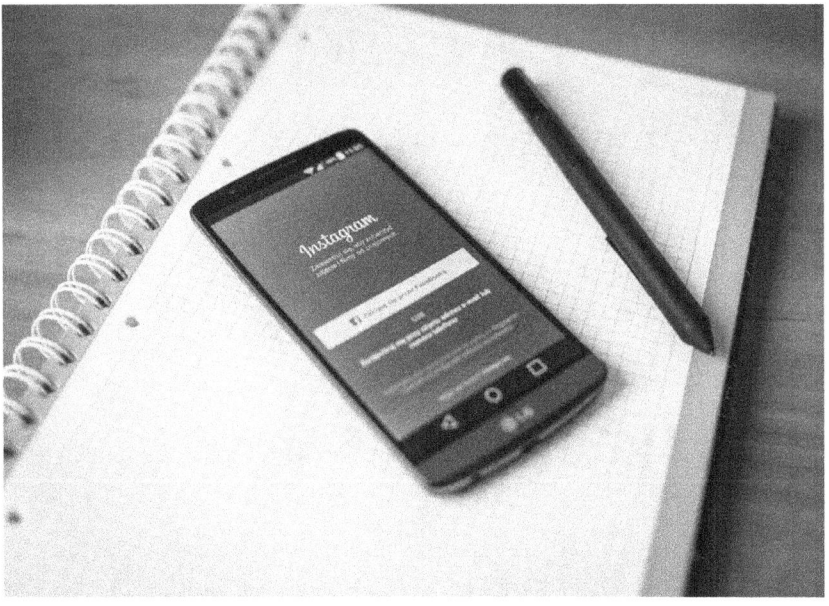

The primary goal of you getting on Instagram is to start earning money as a perfect influencer, so naturally, you are going to want to know how you can actually get into the practice of earning money from your account.

The biggest thing new influencers struggle with, aside from growing their accounts, is getting their followers to become customers, which is necessary if you are going to make any money.

Getting your followers to buy from you takes some practice, consistency, and a few strategies that will help you make sure that you are promoting yourself effectively so that you are likely to actually earn money from your account.

Each influencer is going to have a slightly different relationship with their audience compared to any other influencer out there so, on one level, you are going to need to be willing to adapt your plan to ensure that it actually fits your audience.

However, the general strategies for getting your account profitable and turning your followers into buyers is going to be the same for everyone at its core.

In order to really transition your followers into customers, you are going to have to know what compels them to buy, and then you are going to have to shape your relationships with them in such a way that they are actually compelled to purchase from you.

If you do this correctly, then you will have a highly profitable influencer account that supports you with reaching all of your profit goals on Instagram.

Turning Followers Into Buyers

In general, people need you to understand one thing about them in order to get to buy from them, and they need to have three things in order to actually make the purchase.

The one thing you need to understand is that your followers will buy based on their *emotions*. In fact, their entire loyalty to you is going to be based on their emotions.

If you can provoke your followers to share an emotional connection with you, they will be far more likely to remain loyal to you and to buy from you when you begin sharing sponsored content.

The reason why emotions are so important is because the entire industry of advertising is based on emotional connection, and, with influencers, the key focus is on having an emotional connection between you and your followers.

Then, you use that emotional connection to share things with them, and their loyalty to you has them willing to actually buy what you have shared with them, assuming it is something they will want or need in their lives and they can see the quality and value in it.

Based on this information, the three things your followers need to have before they will buy from you is trust, interest, and excitement.

Your followers need to trust in you, which can be done through sharing an honest emotional relationship with your followers.

You can achieve this by sharing personal parts of your lives with them, responding to their comments and messages, and commenting on their content, too.

Interest is built by sharing products that your followers are actually likely to be interested in, which can be gauged based on what they talk about and what industry you are in. Generally speaking, if you are highly interested, your followers will likely be interested, too, since they are following you for that very reason.

Lastly, you need your followers to be excited. If you are promoting the same things that every other influencer is promoting, your followers are going to grow bored with your content because they feel as though they have already seen it before. You can build excitement in two ways: through *what* you share, and through *how* you share it.

Always do your best to share things that are trendy and unique, and avoid jumping on the train of promoting the exact same thing that everyone else is promoting. While it is perfectly fine to promote popular brands, make sure you have plenty of unique stuff in there, too.

Then, make sure you gauge how your audience responds to things and present these sponsored shares in such a way that gets them excited and eager to try those products out for themselves.

If you successfully build trust, interest, and excitement in your followers, you are going to have an easy time selling to them.

Over time, your followers will grow used to relying on you for great product or service recommendations, and you will likely find yourself experiencing far more success in your sales rates because of it.

With that being said: use your sponsorship deals to continue building trust, interest, and excitement by only making deals with brands *you* trust, are interested in, and get excited by.

Creating Your Instagram Marketing Strategy

When it comes to marketing, strategies give you a clear sense of direction. With the right strategy, you will be far more likely to reach the right people and increase your chances at creating the impact you desire to create with your Instagram profile.

Having a marketing strategy starts with having a well-crafted profile and a clear understanding of how each part of Instagram works together to create the overall user experience. After that, you have to decide how you are going to use each element of the platform to weave together an experience for your followers.

This experience should entice them, increase their interest in you, give them plenty of different forms of content to view, and draw them into your sales funnel, which we will talk more about later.

The first part of your strategy is going to be identifying what your goals are with Instagram, and what your purpose is for being on the platform. At this point, you have already defined your goals, so I want you to recall those goals and make sure that you remain absolutely clear on what they are while you build your strategy.

As an influencer, your primary objective should always be to build a highly engaged community, as a highly engaged community is one that will be far more likely to loyally follow you and buy what you promote. If this is not already a part of your goal, add it to your goal now so that it can be a part of your strategy.

Now, you want to think about who your audience is and what type of content they generally like to consume. The more you can invest in understanding your audience, the more you are going to be able to provide them with plenty of great content that they enjoy and come back for on a regular basis. If you really nail your strategy, they will bring their friends, too.

Once you know what type of content it is that your followers like to consume, you need to strategize ways that you are going to create that content for them. For example, if you find that your audience prefers behind the scenes content, you need to strategize using your stories, and live video feeds as a way to connect with them in a more personalized manner.

You may also prefer to use videos over flat pictures on your feed so that you can create more content that your followers are interested in seeing.

If, however, your followers prefer reading, you may prefer to write more of your content and include written content in your stories, too, so they are more likely to read what you have shared. You may also want to do some videos but always make sure you caption them so that your followers who prefer reading can connect with you in a more personal way while still consuming that content through reading, given that this may be their preference.

No matter what method you use for delivering content to your audience, you need to have two things in place: consistency and modesty.

Consistently uploading new content ensures you stay relevant and continue to nurture your relationship with your audience every single day, which is a necessary step in growing your social media page.

Modesty is an important topic that not a lot of people talk about when it comes to sharing your content on social media. Modesty does not mean that you are not vulnerable or open with your audience, but it does mean that you are not sharing too much at once.

Rather than giving 5 beauty tips in one video, for example, break those beauty tips out over 5 days. Or, rather than throwing up 3-4 different dietary tips in a post or a story, make those 3-4 separate posts over 2-4 days, depending on your content calendar.

Being modest and breaking everything down into bite-sized pieces means your audience is way more likely to read it *and* that they are going to be way more likely to come back to get more tips from you in the following days.

Aside from these parts of your strategy, there are three additional steps you need to take to finalize your marketing strategy. These include: having a clear call to action, plotting and perfecting your sales funnel, and generating sales through increasing attention on your page.

We are going to discuss each of these three strategies in greater detail below.

Having a Solid Call to Action

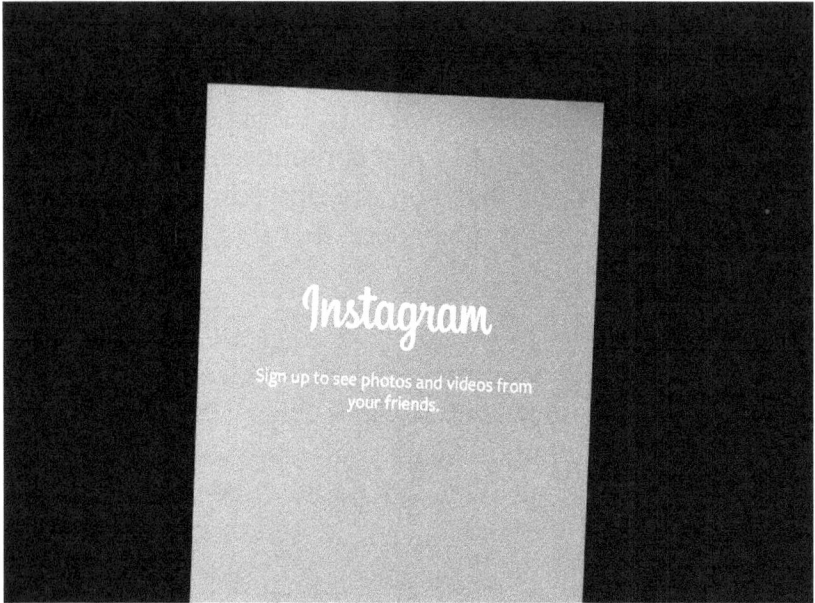

Once you convert your Instagram page to a business page, you are going to have a call to action button you can use to generate a specific result from your page. This could result in people messaging you, visiting your website, booking a service with you, or engaging in any other interaction with you, depending on what you are looking for.

You should adjust your call to action button by going to your business profile, selecting "edit profile" and tapping "contact options." There, tap "add an action button" and select whatever call to action button you want displayed on your page.

You should not rely exclusively on your call to action button to do all of the work for you, though. A strong Instagram marketing plan will include a call to action in each of your posts, too. Every single call to action you use should, in one way or another, lead to your main call to action, which should be one that either increases loyalty or gains sales.

With that being said, you should not repeat the exact same call to action over and over again as people will get bored of it and will stop engaging with you.

To create your call to action, finish each post with a request or a question. Saying something like, "Don't you agree?" "What is your experience with this?" "Book a session to find out more!" "Get the answer on my blog." or something similar gives your audience a clear prompt to follow.

This way, if they were engaged with your post, they will be engaged with your call to action and they will follow through, allowing you to increase your engagement and drive more traffic through your sales funnel.

Creating a Sales Funnel on Instagram

Even as an influencer, you are going to have a deep need for a sales funnel. A sales funnel draws people through your profile with an intentionally mapped out experience that ultimately leads to them landing on an opportunity to buy something from you, or through you. Every single post you make on Instagram, whether it's an inline post, an IGTV post, a story post, or a live video, should all drive people through your sales funnel.

To do so, you want to offer something and then create a call to action at the end of your post that drives them through your sales funnel so that they will go to the next step of it.

On Instagram, people's attention is relatively short-lived so you are going to want to make sure your sales funnel is complete in 3 clicks or less. For example, your follower finds you, finds a post, and then clicks the link to purchase a product that you are promoting.

This is great. Short sales funnel that quickly drive people from your content to your offer so that you can get paid.

The easiest way to do this is to have one "main post" that promotes something. You can refresh that main post daily or every few days, typically depending on your contract with the company you are affiliated with, as well as your content calendar. That main post can either be a post you make that talks about the offer or an IGTV video that you make that talks about the offer.

You can make both, but ideally, you should choose just one to be the "main post" and the other will direct viewers to that post. Then, every other form of content you make should drive people to that post in an authentic way, so whenever it is relevant to what you are actively posting about.

For example, if your main post is an IGTV video, you could make a post and a few stories talking about said product and then direct people over to the IGTV video to learn more.

Alternatively, if your main post is a post, you could use IGTV videos and story feeds to direct people to that main post. If people land on the main post first, their time spent in the sales funnel is simply shorter than the others'.

The main post itself should always drive people directly to the product you are promoting so that they can immediately buy whatever it is that you have talked about. If you are not actively promoting a product, you can promote your blog as a means to get people to sign up for your email list. Or, you could get them to go follow you. This is a great way to increase your attention and make it so that you have even more people to build relationships with and market to in the future.

Generating Sales and Going Viral

Generating sales and going viral is as simple as creating consistent content and staying committed to your sales funnel.

The more you can put content out there, engage with your followers, build the relationship you share with them, and offer high-quality content, the more viewers you are going to get.

With that being said, there are two other things you can do to increase your likelihood of going viral.

The first thing is to make sure that you are always creating content that is highly enjoyable and that people are going to be likely to want to share. If you can create highly enjoyable content, people are going to be far more likely to have fun with it and rewatch it, as well as show other people.

The second thing you can do is share it in as many places as possible, and encourage your followers to do the same.

Have them tag their friends, share it with your blog or your story feed, share it to Twitter, Facebook and any other platform you have, and do your best to really get your content out there.

The more consistent you are with sharing it and increasing your audience, as well as making enjoyable content, the more likely you will be to go viral. As well, the more attention you are building and the more fun you are having, the better your relationships with people will be and the more likely you will be to earn sales.

Affiliate Marketing Strategies

Affiliate marketing works exactly the same as any other marketing strategy, except that you are going to need to adhere to the guidelines of whatever deal it is that you have made with an affiliate marketing company.

Often, these details will be defined in advance and should be agreed to before you ever commit to doing the deal in the first place. Once you know what is expected of you, such as how many posts you should make and what type of things you should say, you can start incorporating that into your marketing strategy.

Never take a deal that you cannot easily and authentically incorporate into your marketing strategy as this can result in your followers thinking you were only in it for the money, which can drastically reduce their trust in you and therefore your bottom line.

Instead, as soon as you know what the final deal will be looking like at your content calendar and your brand guidelines and see how you can work that deal into your own strategy.

If you can reasonably do so, you can go ahead and take the deal and start incorporating it into your marketing plan. Simply fit it into your content calendar and build a sales funnel around that post as many times per your agreement and you will have the simplest and most effective sales funnel available.

Common Mistakes to Avoid

When it comes to marketing on Instagram, the number one mistake you must avoid is coming across as insincere or ingenuine.

People on Instagram are marketed to every day and, in most cases, they enjoy learning about new businesses and products and have no problem being marketed to on a consistent basis.

The problem comes in when they begin to realize that the people marketing to them are ingenuine and are only there for the money. They already know that you are in it for the money, and they are often more than happy to pay for products or services *when* they can tell that you are authentic and passionate about what it is that you are sharing.

For that reason, never start a business that you cannot be absolutely passionate about because it will destroy your reputation and prevent you from creating the results you desire.

As well, avoid coming across as spammy. Sometimes, a large amount of passion can translate to excitement, and that excitement can have you being *too* active on the platform.

While it is good to engage and share with your audience, sharing too much content too often can result in people unfollowing you because you start to dominate their newsfeed.

They want to see the other accounts, too, so be mindful of that when you are taking up space on their newsfeed.

Conclusion

Getting on Instagram and starting out as an influencer is an exciting choice to make, especially when you realize that, in doing so, you gain the opportunity to create your own business and your own hours.

Many influencers have fun living their passion and partnering with brands they care about, which is what makes this particular path so enjoyable.

With that being said, many people do find that when they first start out as an influencer, it can be somewhat uncomfortable and even embarrassing. It is not unusual to feel weird about self-promotion and all of the work that comes with growing your influencer account; however it does get easier with time.

The more you practice self-promotion, grow confident in your marketing strategy, and receive positive feedback from your audience, the easier it is to grow your influencer account.

One of the biggest pieces of advice I want to give you before you go is to keep going and never give up.

If you choose something you are truly passionate about and you keep trying over and over again, you are sure to find yourself creating an amazing career as an influencer.

Some influencers found that it took 1-3 years of consistent posting for them to create the results they desired, but it does not have to take that long for you. Continue building great content, refining your strategy, and doing what you can to get your name out there, and in time, you will find yourself rocking an amazing Instagram influencer brand.

Remember, Instagram itself is a social media platform, which means it is designed to create an enjoyable user experience. The more you can focus on leveraging that user experience to design your personal brand experience for your followers, the more likely you will be to create the results you desire with your account.

You want to continue working within the benefits and features of Instagram to create a stronger and more enjoyable experience so that more and more people follow you.

As they do, you become more valuable to potential brands and, as a result, you find yourself creating strong relationships with those brands.

The relationships you share with brands combined with the relationships you share with your followers will result in you earning an excellent living off of your Instagram influencer business.

In order to really stay at the top of your game, be sure to continue paying attention to Instagram updates in their features and algorithms as they update their platform every so often.

This platform is always creating new ways to interact with your audience and refining their algorithm to improve the user experience.

Staying on top of what they are doing allows you to continue to work with the algorithm, rather than trying to work against it to build a brand. Building in harmony is a far better way to succeed than trying to fight against the platform itself.

Lastly, if you feel that *Instagram Influencer and Advertising: A Social Media Marketing Guide Book, Grow Your Personal Brand and Become A Perfect Influencer* by me, Joan Smith, has supported you in growing your influencer account, I ask that you, please take a moment to review my book on Amazon Kindle. Your honest feedback will help me create more great guide books to support you in your climb to success.

Thank you, and best of luck in becoming an influencer! Remember, stay consistent and focus on building strong relationships with your followers. The more you do, the more likely you will be to create the powerhouse of a brand you desire and deserve.

*"Did this book help you in some way?
If so, I'd love to hear about it.*

*Honest reviews help readers find the right
book for their needs."*